THE FIRST DOGS

The dog family lived on Earth for millions of years before Man arrived. They were long-tailed, short-legged, meat-eating, ferocious little creatures who preyed on the leaf-eating animals and attacked them. These fierce animals, called **Miacis**, were the great ancestors of all dogs, both tame and wild, that we know today.

No-one knows how men and dogs first became friends.

Men soon discovered that dogs helped them to hunt for food, and that dogs also helped to protect them.

Dogs are friendly animals and they found they got more protection and food living with Man.

Millions of years later, about 10,000 years ago, Man met his first dog. They became friends, and have been working, hunting and playing together ever since.

Today dogs still work on farms, mountains and moorlands herding cattle and sheep. They are still invaluable to hunters and to the police for tracking criminals.

Today dogs are also to be seen in exhibition rings, films, television, famous paintings, plays and circuses. Hundreds of dog books have been written. Thousands of people earn their living by breeding dogs. Factories have been built to produce dog biscuits, tins of dog food, dog kennels, dog collars and dog toys.

Today, as it has always been, a dog's greatest role is still as a faithful friend and companion to people both young and old all over the world.

CHOOSING YOUR DOG

Think carefully before you choose your dog, and try to answer some of these questions before you do.

Does everybody else at home want a dog too?

Can you afford to feed him and pay the vet's bills?

Is your home the right place for him? Will he fit into it? Will you get bored with him after the novelty of having a dog wears off? Do you have time to prepare his meals, give him a daily brush, walk him for at least an hour each day, maybe for the next fifteen years? Will your mother be prepared to do all this when your father is at work and you are at school?

What is to be done with your dog when you go on holiday?

The next thing you have to think about is what sort of dog you want – there is a wide choice. Over thousands of years, men have developed different types or **breeds** of dog to do special jobs. These breeds can be put into six main **groups** of dogs that are officially recognised in the world today. The six groups are: **Sporting dogs**, **Hounds**, **Working dogs**, **Terriers**, **Non-sporting dogs**, and **Toy dogs**. There is also a seventh unofficial group caused by accidental breeding – the loveable **mongrel**.

PURE BREDS OR MONGRELS?

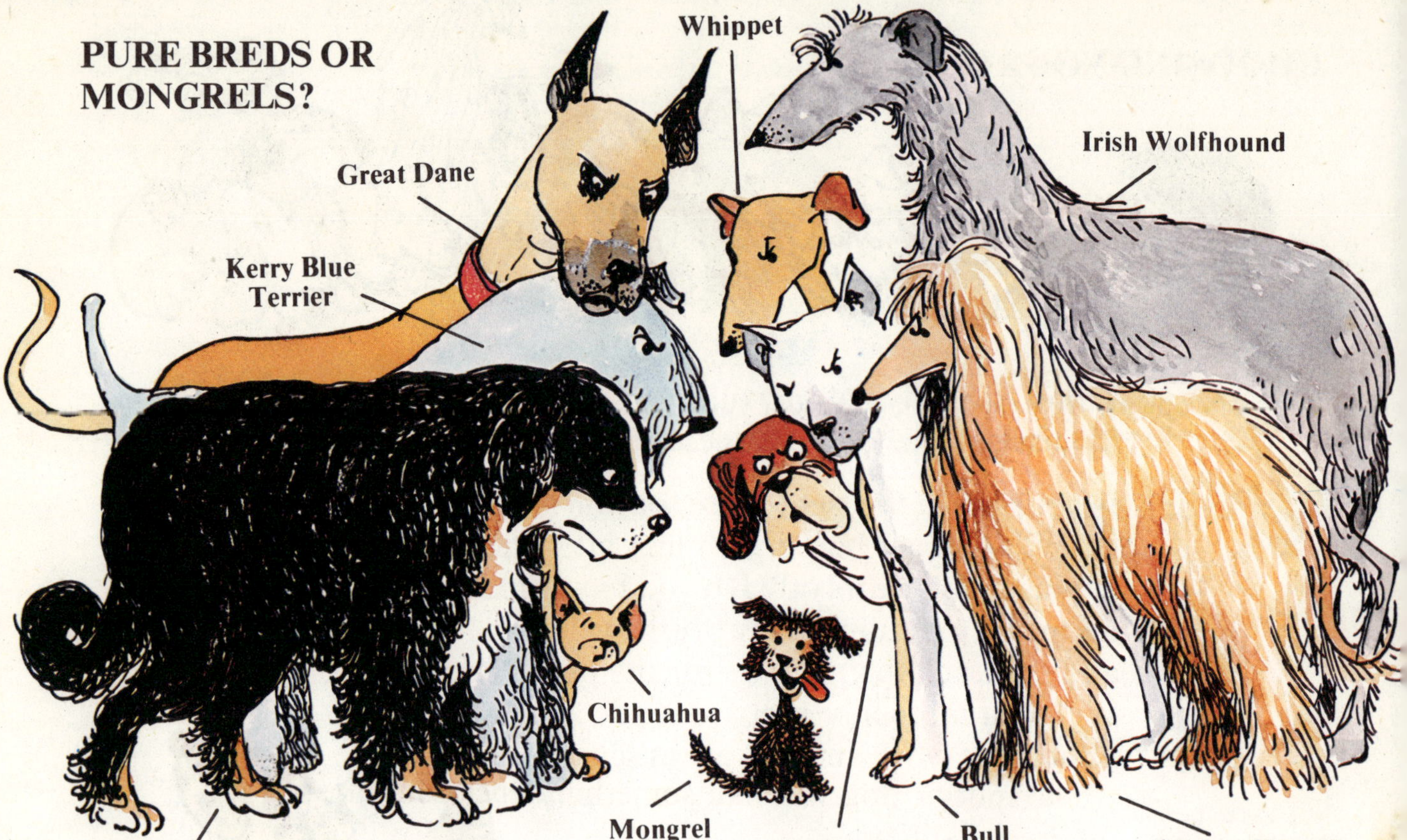

Whippet
Great Dane
Irish Wolfhound
Kerry Blue Terrier
Chihuahua
Mongrel
Bernese Mountain Dog
American Foxhound
Bull Terrier
Afghan Hound

Each breed of dog has particular characteristics in their build, personality and needs which may help you to choose the right one for you. There are dogs to suit every taste – big dogs, little dogs, lively dogs, quiet dogs, frail dogs and dogs as solid as a rock. If you have a pure-bred puppy you should have a good idea of the sort of dog it will grow up to be.

With a mongrel or cross-bred puppy, you are less likely to know how it will develop as its parents do not belong to the same breed – and very likely its grandparents and great grandparents did not either. However, mongrels are often as friendly, intelligent and great hearted as dogs of ancient pedigree.

On the following pages are all the groups of dogs and information on how to keep **your** dog healthy and happy, whatever its breed.

Whippet
Mongrel
Basset Hound

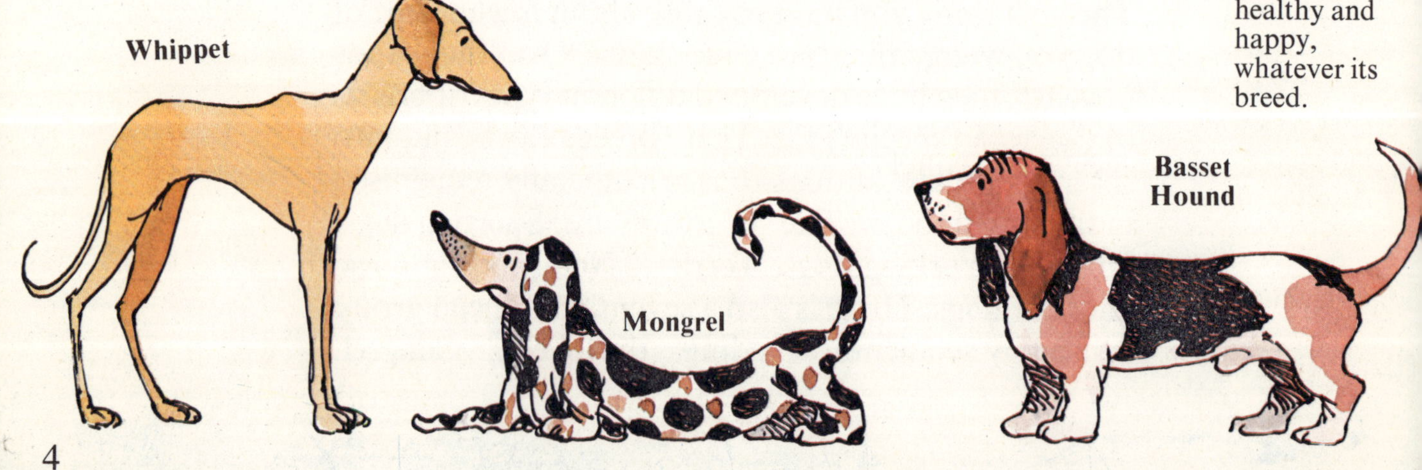

THE HOUSING PROBLEM

Once owner and dog have chosen each other, the next question is, where will he sleep?

The indoor dog will like something enclosed, like a basket or a box, with a blanket to keep out the draughts. He will probably go there when he is ready for bed, or when the hoover is out or when he wants to be left alone. This is his place of refuge.

If your dog is very big or has to live outside, he will need a good weatherproof kennel with the floor and doorway well clear of the ground (but not too far!)

TRAINING YOUR DOG

When you first get your dog let him make himself at home. Let him get used to his surroundings and the people he is going to live with. The greatest thing of all at this time is to establish his confidence.

Roll him over on his back and stroke his tummy. He will like that.

Training your puppy takes time. It is a gradual process, and should become easier as your friendship grows.

Then begin to teach him his name.

HERE,-LLANFAIRPWLL GWYNGYLL-
-GOGERYCHWYRNDROBWLL-
-LLANTYSILIOGOGOGOCH!!!
?

Something short and snappy is best.

Dogs can get confused if their names are long.

HOUSE TRAINING

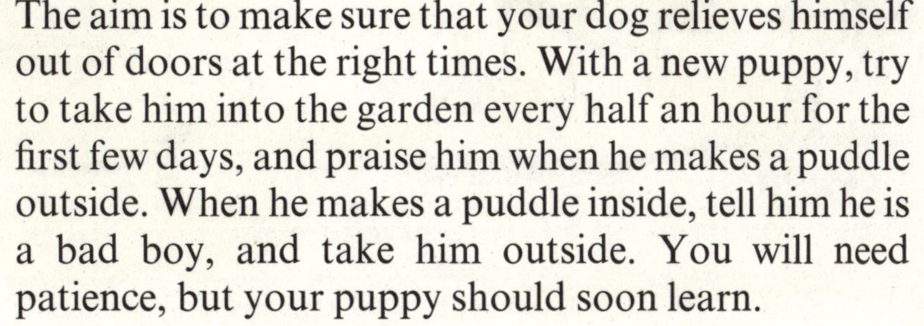

The aim is to make sure that your dog relieves himself out of doors at the right times. With a new puppy, try to take him into the garden every half an hour for the first few days, and praise him when he makes a puddle outside. When he makes a puddle inside, tell him he is a bad boy, and take him outside. You will need patience, but your puppy should soon learn.

Soon your puppy will ask to go out. Keep an eye open for the signs.

Simple commands like bed, sit, heel, stay and good boy should be given in a clear, firm but friendly voice. If he has done wrong, a gentle tap and 'no' or 'bad boy' given in a slightly gruff voice, will do. A small tit-bit can be offered as a reward to coax him into doing what you want.

Don't tire your puppy when training him. 10 minutes is long enough for a session, or you could try two 5 minute sessions.

FEEDING

An eight week puppy should have four small meals a day.

Two meals should be of fish or meat cut into small pieces and mixed with puppy meal or brown bread, and some greens.

The other two meals can be either milk, or milk and egg, poured over puppy meal or a little cereal.

Although tinned food contains a well-balanced diet for your dog, you must also give him fresh food regularly.

Your dog relies on **YOU** to give him food and drink.

After six months he can have two meals and a snack, and after nine months, just one meal and a snack. The quantities get larger as he grows.

You will need to watch your dog during the first few months to see which food he likes and dislikes, and which food does not agree with him.

You also need to vary his food otherwise he will get bored with it.

Ignore your dog if he begs at the table.

Feed your dog at regular times. He will learn, and not let you forget, when he should be given his meals.

Watch your dog eat to find out how much food to give him. He should eat energetically but not greedily. If he leaves anything he is either ill or has been given too much, so you need to watch him at his next meal. When he has finished eating, remove his food bowl.

Always have a bowl of water out for your dog to drink.

Don't give him too many sweets. They will make his teeth bad.

When a dog is getting too fat he wants two things – more exercise and less food!

Chicken and fish bones are bad for dogs as they splinter and may get stuck in their throats.

A puppy shouldn't leave his own garden until he has had injections against two serious dog illnesses, hard pad and distemper.

Puppies usually have these inoculations at 3 months.

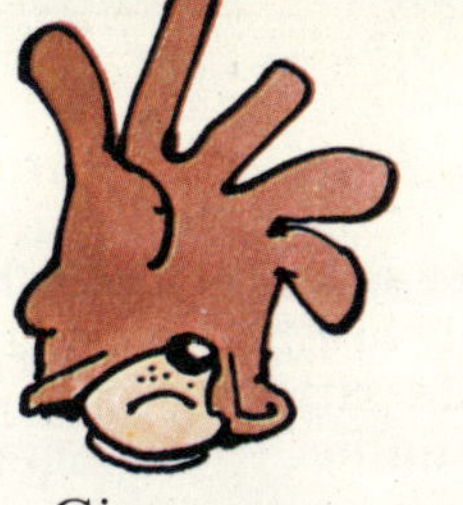

Give your puppy some toys to play with. An old glove and ball will do.

Your puppy has to learn to wear a collar and lead.

Don't rush him. Don't try to teach him too soon.

You will soon learn your dog's dislikes, and when you need to keep a tight hold on the lead.

EXERCISE

Dogs are active creatures, but if left on their own by a fire, they will get lazy and unfit. A wise dog owner will take his dog for regular exercise. Try to take him for a long walk twice a day. If possible, let him off the lead for a good run. If you don't live in the country, you are bound to find a park or a common, or some open space for him to run in.

When you are walking near traffic, keep your dog on a lead. Walk well away from the kerb.

Take a ball or a stick for him to fetch. And remember, if you are walking near water, dogs love to swim.

Be careful of: cliff tops, quarries, broken glass and barbed wire.

Try and find walks where your dog can run free.

You will be amazed how many open spaces you can find in a city. It is a great way to explore your neighbourhood.

When out walking in the country make sure he doesn't worry sheep or cattle. If he does, he may get shot by the farmer.

GROOMING YOUR DOG

Groom your puppy on the first day so that his daily brush becomes part of his routine.

Start him off with a soft brush. You can use a comb on him when his coat thickens.

Be quiet, sensible and cautious when you brush him. Your puppy should enjoy his grooming.

Check your dog's general condition every day. This will help you to get to know your dog so that you can quickly see if anything is wrong.

Brushing is very important because it keeps your dog's skin in good condition.

Most dogs enjoy being groomed. With most dogs you should brush the way of the hair from the crown of the head to the tail, and then down the sides and chest.

The easiest type of brush to use is oval with a hand strap.

Smooth-coated dogs can be groomed much more quickly using a firm-bristled brush.

Grooming is also important because you will quickly find out if your dog has fleas or lice, or has a sore or a rash.

You should brush your dog every day, regularly check up on his teeth, and occasionally give him a bath. You don't need to overdo it, but grooming is important if you want to keep your dog healthy and comfortable.

Brush your dog more frequently when he is moulting.

This removes the loose, dead hair which tends to get everywhere.

You will have to be careful if your dog has a very long coat to get the tangles out without hurting him.

YOUR DOG'S HEALTH

Teeth

Keep a regular check on his teeth.

With a full-grown dog, a marrow bone acts as a very good toothbrush.

If your dog has stains on his teeth, you can remove them by dipping some cotton wool in some bicarbonate of soda dissolved in water and rubbing them.

The easiest way to do this is to hold the dog between your knees, hold his muzzle, lift his lip and rub.

Ears and Eyes

NEVER poke in his ears with anything pointed or hard.

Look into his ears and, if needed, sponge them with a tissue and some warm water.

Also check your dog's eyes. If the corner of his eye is messy, wipe it very carefully with a tissue.

Always throw away immediately the tissues you have used to clean your dog's ears or eyes.

Nails and Paws

If your dog does not get regular road walks his toe nails may need attention.

The nails should be filed not cut. If you are not sure what to do or how to do it, see the vet.

Grooming is a very good time to check your dog's health.

Be careful of his nose and eyes.

Look out for fleas or other insects, and for any sores or rashes on your dog's skin.

ILLNESS

In some countries, like Australia, dogs need to be checked and powdered **every** day in the summer months. Bites from the ticks there can **kill** a dog!

Your dog's health is very important. A healthy dog **looks** healthy. The better you get to know your dog, the quicker you will be able to tell if he is off colour and unwell. You must keep an eye on his appearance, his behaviour and his droppings.

If your dog has fleas, dust him all over with a good flea powder (ask your local pet shop) and then brush him.

If you see that your dog is limping have a look at his paw.

He may have a thorn in it or a piece of grit.

Gently clean it with a little warm water with some antiseptic added

and try to remove the thorn with a pair of tweezers.

If you cannot remove the thorn, or if he has a bad cut of swelling, **TAKE YOUR DOG TO THE VET**.

NEVER ignore it. The limp won't just go away.

Other danger signs to watch out for are a dry nose, dribbling, discharge from the nostrils, lumps, swellings and watery eyes.

Be very careful what you leave around the house that your dog may eat. Also be careful of fires and wires he may chew.

If you have to give your dog medicine this is one way of getting him to take it.

Hold him between your knees. Take his muzzle with one hand and insert the pill or medicine into the side of his mouth.

Tilt the head back, still holding his muzzle, and gently stroke his throat until he swallows it.

A comfortable warm bed, water to drink, food and loving attention will soon get him back on his legs.

If your dog is unwell, take him to see the vet. If he is very unwell, the vet will come to you. The best thing you can do is nurse him carefully through his sickness. Good nursing can do wonders for a sick dog as it does for humans.

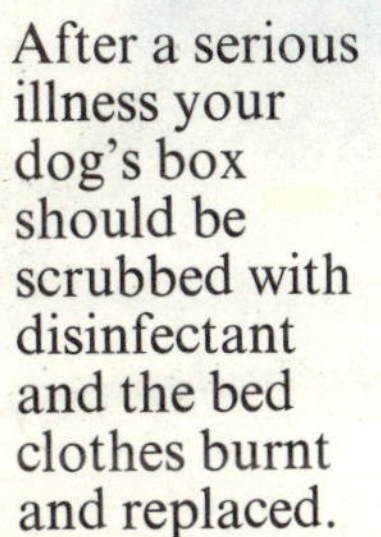

After a serious illness your dog's box should be scrubbed with disinfectant and the bed clothes burnt and replaced.

Love and care for your dog, and you will have a loyal and affectionate friend for many years.

YOUR DOG AND THE LAW

After your dog is 6 months old he will need a licence.

You can obtain this from your local Post Office.

You have to renew your licence every year.

Don't forget!

He should wear a collar with your name and address attached to it.

This is very important if he gets lost.

You are now responsible for your dog's behaviour.

Your dog mustn't attack anyone going about their lawful business.

You can be held responsible if your dog damages any sheep, cattle, horses or poultry.

It is illegal to **urge** a dog to bite, attack or frighten any person or animal.

All road accidents in which your dog is involved must be reported to the police.

In many public parks your dog must be kept on a lead.

Check the notices when you go in.

Dogs cannot be brought into some countries, for example, Great Britain, without first undergoing a period of quarantine.

This is an important precaution against a deadly disease called **Rabies**.

The smuggling of animals into a country with quarantine laws is a very serious offence.

It is your duty to train your dog properly and care for him all through his life.

You will be repayed, over and over again, by his companionship, devotion and love.

THE DOG SHOW . . . . . . AND FIELD TRIAL

Ever since early cavemen domesticated the dog, men have compared **their** dog with everyone elses, to see who had the best dog.

Today, very competitive Dog Shows and Field Trials take place.

A lot of money can be made by the owners of the dogs that win.

Field Trial

Field Trials are held, literally, out in the fields and woods. In them, the Sporting dogs and the Working dogs show how well-trained they are at their work. The dog's intelligence and the way he solves problems are very important in a Field Trial.

There is always a great demand for the puppies of a winner.

Dog Show

A Dog Show is held to find the best dog in each breed. Kennel Clubs all over the world have a set of standards that has been laid down for each breed, and the dogs in a show are tested to see which dog has the best standard.

Dog Shows are very popular with breeders and owners, not only for the prizes, but also because they help keep the standards of the breeds high.

Dog Shows also help to change the popularity of the breeds from year to year.

Dogs must walk at their owner's sides, come to heel, sit, stay and learn to be quiet and calm with other dogs.

The training for this can benefit both owner and dog as they must both learn to co-operate with each other.

Your dog can learn to respond to your wishes very quickly, and this is tested in obedience trials at Dog Shows.

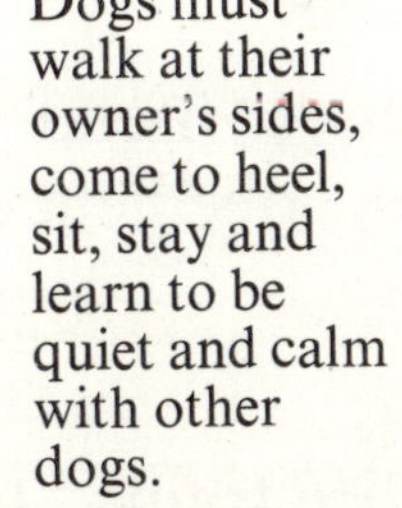

This training is important outside the Dog Show, in daily life. It is also great fun!

THE DOG GROUPS AND BREEDS

SPORTING DOGS

Sporting dogs can be divided into four smaller groups each with a special skill to do with hunting: **Pointers, Setters, Spaniels** and **Retrievers**.

Pointer

A Pointer will 'freeze' with his nose pointing in a bird's direction so the hunter can find it easily.

Setter

A Setter will do the same but will 'point' sitting on his haunches, sometimes for hours, until the hunter arrives to flush the bird into the air.

Sporting dogs are active, friendly and faithful, and when well trained make obedient companions.

Pointers and Setters

Pointers and Setters are trained to hunt birds. They find, by smell, where the bird is hiding.

Red Setter

There are **English, Irish** and **Gordon Setters.**

Spaniels

There are many kinds of Spaniels including the **English Cocker** and **American Cocker Spaniel**; **Irish Water**, **Springer**, and **Field** and **Sussex Spaniels**.

Spaniels work very closely with the hunter and remain in his sight.

Their job in the hunting field is to run ahead of their masters and flush the game out into the open.

After the shot, they remain motionless until told to fetch the 'game'.

Cocker Spaniel

Retrievers

There are **Curly-coated**, **Flat-coated** and **Golden Retrievers**, and **Retriever Labradors**.

The Retriever's job is to return the game to the hunter's feet without harming it with its teeth.

Retrievers have a very soft mouth so that they don't mark the bird.

Retrievers wait patiently with the hunter in cover until he shoots the game.

Because of their intelligence, gentleness and obedience, Labradors can be trained to make excellent guide-dogs for the blind.

Sometimes they have to swim very long distances to 'retrieve' the game.

Golden Retriever

HOUNDS

Hounds are solidly-built dogs who like running and tracking. They were bred for hunting deer, fox and rabbit. Hounds will chase, trap and hold an animal in one place until the hunters arrive for the kill.

There are two types of Hounds, **Sight Hounds** and **Scent Hounds**.

Sight Hounds

Sight Hounds are, historically, the oldest group of dogs used by man.

All Hounds are self-willed, independent, faithful, somewhat stubborn, affectionate with their owners, but aloof with strangers.

Afghan

The **Saluki**, **Afghan**, **Greyhound**, **Borzoi**, and **Irish Wolfhound** are all Sight Hounds.

The Irish Wolfhound is the largest of all dogs, growing as tall as 86 cm. Despite their size they are very gentle dogs who love children.

Most Sight Hounds have long, graceful legs, slim bodies and pointed noses.

The exception is the short-legged **Dachshund** which was used to hunt small game.

They can run and jump with great speed and agility and vault over streams, hedges and walls, and still have the strength to go on.

Don't forget this when taking him for a walk!

Irish Wolfhound

Scent Hounds

These dogs have an extremely fine sense of smell, and track game by following the scent along the ground.

Scent Hounds are an ancient group of dogs. The **Basenji** was used by the Ancient Egyptian Pharaohs; the **Beagle** was found in Ancient Rome; the **Basset** in early England, and the **Elkhound** goes back to 5000 B.C.

The **Foxhound**, **Otter Hound** and **American Coonhound** are also Scent Hounds.

Bloodhound

The Bloodhound is the best example of a Scent Hound.

They are used by the police for tracking down escaped criminals.

A Bloodhound can follow a track many days old, and track it for many kilometres.

The record is 222 kilometres.

Bloodhound

TERRIERS

The name **Terrier** comes from the Latin word **Terra**, meaning Earth, as these dogs were bred to go underground after their prey.

Being small, Terriers don't need much exercise, and they have small appetites.

However, there are some exceptions!

Terriers are bold, courageous little dogs with a will of their own. They are friendly and loyal and make loveable companions.

Terriers are popular as pets because they are small and well suited to living in towns.

There are many different kinds of Terriers. Some have short, smooth coats and others have rough, curly ones.

Terriers are lively and playful dogs, and fond of playing with children.

They are nearly all small dogs who have a lot of courage.

Welsh, American Staffordshire, Australian, Border, **Fox, Cairn, Skye** and **West Highland** are some more members of the Terrier family.

At dog shows, Terrier classes are very popular and well attended. If you wish to 'show' your Terrier he will require a lot of grooming.

A daily brush and trim twice a year will do nicely for a house-pet, but for a show dog it is quite different.

Prolonged grooming is essential, and should start long before the show begins, and continue until the moment the dog enters the ring.

Dalmatian

The Dalmatian has a number of names: the **Fire House Dog, Plum Pudding Dog**, and **Coach Dog**.

They were bred as coach dogs to follow the old horse-drawn carriages for long distances, and guard them from robbers and bandits.

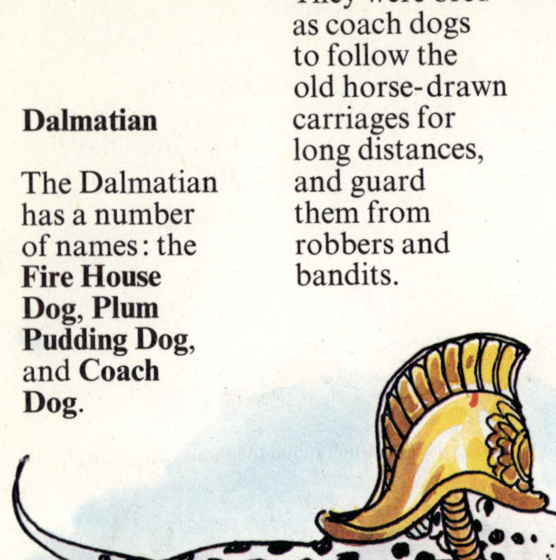

Dalmatians get on well with horses, and were often kept as pets by the early horse-drawn fire engine teams.

Dalmatian

They are strong, active dogs, and they are very intelligent.

They learn easily, are good with children and they are also good watch-dogs.

Dalmatians have an unusual, spotted coat.

Puppies are born with a white coat, and the spots develop quite quickly.

NON-SPORTING DOGS

The group, **Non-sporting dogs**, contains rather a mixture of dogs. Breeds of dog which are difficult to classify are usually put into this group.

Non-sporting dogs were originally bred for special purposes, **Bulldogs** for baiting bulls, **Dalmatians** to accompany carriages, but they are now kept as pets.

Bulldogs, **Boston Terriers**, **Tibetan Terriers**, the **Schipperke** and **Lhasa Apso** are also in the Non-sporting group.

Chow Chow

The Chow Chow, now a popular pet, was used in ancient China as a guard dog, hunter and retriever.

The Chow Chow is the only dog to have a blue-black tongue.

Chow Chow

They are independent, stubborn, aloof, courageous and very loyal.

They have a beautiful, very thick coat and look like lions.

In Northern China the Chow Chow is also used as a sleigh dog.

The Poodle

The Poodle has a very long history and is one of the most popular pets today.

Poodles were bred as working dogs and have been used as sheepdogs, gundogs, watch dogs and retrievers.

They are very intelligent dogs with a 'sense of humour', and they are easily trained.

They are often used in performing dog acts, in circuses and on the television.

There are three sizes of Poodle. The **standard** is about 66 cm tall; the **miniature** grows to about 38 cm, and the **toy** to only 25 cm.

Poodles have very thick, long coats which need to be groomed and clipped regularly.

Poodles can be black, brown, cream, white, apricot, silver or grey.

Many cities have 'Poodle Parlours' or 'Beauty Salons For Poodles' where the dogs are groomed and properly clipped.

Some Poodle owners have their dogs dyed bright colours. **NEVER DO THIS TO YOUR DOG**. The dye can irritate its skin.

Whatever dog you have, you should always respect its dignity and intelligence.

TOY DOGS

Toy dogs have been bred for hundreds of years.

During the Middle Ages these dogs would sit on their mistresses' laps to attract the fleas!

Chihuahua

They were mainly bred as pets, but in the Middle Ages they were also used as ratters in the large rat infested halls and castles.

The popularity of **Toy dogs** is not so much for their character, which can be quite aggressive, but because they are so small. Toy dogs make good pets for people who want a dog, but who do not have room for a larger breed.

Ladies of the Court loved to carry them as ornaments.

Toy dogs, although pretty to look at, are hardy dogs, and should not be pampered.

Toy dogs are more suitable as pets for adults than for children.

They are affectionate and loyal, and easily trained.

However small, Toy dogs are true dogs and should be respected as such.

If they are not fed with sweets or carried everywhere, they will live to a ripe old age.

They are lively, intelligent dogs who love to be with people, but they do tend to bark more than other breeds.

Chihuahua

The Chihuahua, thought to have come from Mexico, is the smallest dog in the world.

They are about 10–13 cm high.

Chihuahuas can have either a smooth coat, or a long one. They come in a variety of colours.

Chihuahuas feel the cold, and love to sleep curled up on the end of a bed.

Unfortunately, they tend to snore!

Pekingese

The Pekingese was a sacred dog in ancient China.

They have beautiful coats, with a great mane of hair around their necks.

They are sometimes called Lion Dogs because they are independent, courageous, proud and bold.

Shih Tzu

Shih Tzu is Chinese for lion.

This little dog is active and alert, and loves being with people.

Pug

Pugs are sturdy dogs, who love to please.

Pugs often have breathing problems because their noses are 'squashed'.

Miniature Pinscher

This little German dog is intelligent, playful, sturdy and a good watchdog.

Yorkshire Terrier

Yorkshire Terriers are confident, intelligent dogs.

Their long, silky coats need daily grooming.

Pomeranian

This is a very ancient breed, that gets its name from the Baltic land, Pomerania.

Papillon is the French word for butterfly. The Papillon's ears are high and fringed, and look like a butterfly's open wings.

Sheepdogs

Collies, **Briards**, **Pulis**, **Great Pyrenees**, **Welsh Corgis**, **English** and **Belgian Sheepdogs** all work with sheep.

Dutch Shepherd Dog
English Sheepdog
Berger de Brie
Kuvasz
Welsh Corgi
Alsatian
Collie
Catala Sheepdog
Armant

WORKING DOGS

There are still many dogs today who are not just pets, but serve and work with their owners. These are the **Working dogs**.

Working dogs are very intelligent and when trained, they often work on their own, making decisions and solving problems.

Working dogs can be divided into four smaller groups: **Sheepdogs**, **Guard dogs**, **Sled dogs** and **Service dogs**.

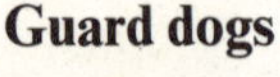

Guard dogs

Guard dogs are used in almost every kind of military and police work.

The **German Shepherd (Alsatian)**, the **Doberman Pinscher** and the **Rottweiler** are all originally from Germany.

They are all very intelligent, fearless, loyal dogs who need to be trained at an early age.

The **Boxer** and the **Great Dane** are also used as Guard dogs. They are also loyal, protective and intelligent. Both of them are aggressive with strangers, but are gentle with children.

Sled dogs

For over 5000 years Sled dogs have worked with man pulling loaded sleds through snow, over long distances, in extremely cold weather.

These dogs have extremely thick coats, with a dense, short undercoat, and a thick, long 'over' coat.

Their coat is oily to make it waterproof.

They can sleep in snow at −45°C (50°F below zero)! Often they will dig themselves into a hole in the snow and curl into a ball with their tail covering their nose.

Eskimo Husky

The **Eskimo Husky**, the **Siberian Husky**, the **Samoyed**, **Alaskan Malamute** and the **Chinese Chow** are all Sled dogs.

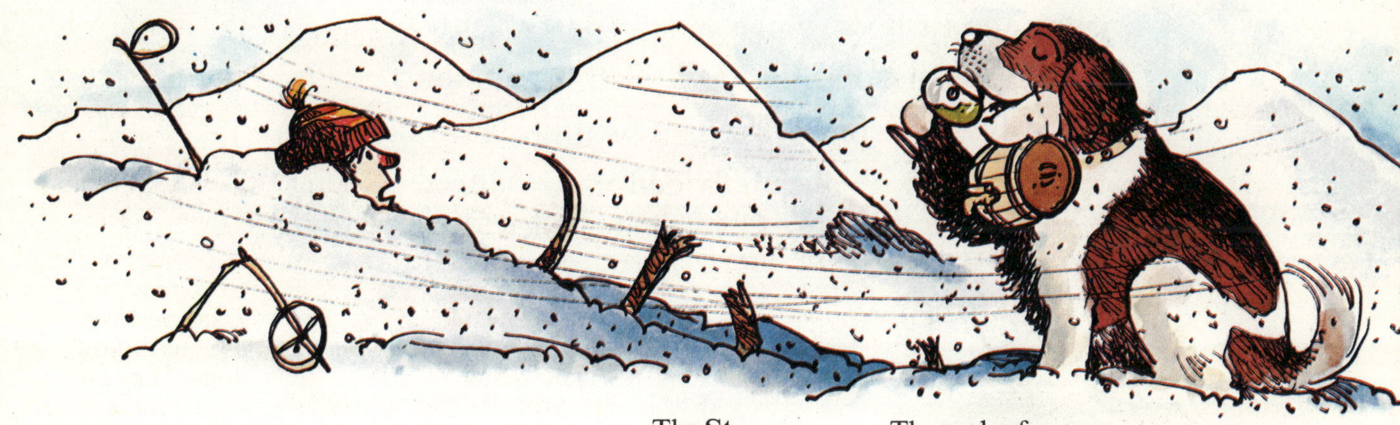

St. Bernard

The **St. Bernard** was bred by the Monks of Saint Bernard in Switzerland to find travellers lost on the mountains.

The cask of brandy round its neck was to help revive the rescued traveller.

Service dogs

Newfoundlands were bred as ship's dogs to work with sea-rescue teams.

They are big, strong dogs who can swim in heavy seas and are used to take a line to a drowning person and tow them to safety.

Newfoundland

The **German Schnauzer** and the **Belgian Bouvier des Flandres** were both used to pull carts.

Since the early caveman made friends with his first dog, a dog's life has been considerably changed.

Dogs have become thoroughly domesticated, and through breeding, they have changed their appearance, their habits, their temperament and even their natural instincts.

In some parts of the world today, there are **still** some wild dogs roaming around, preying on other animals and living the same kind of life that they did before they met Man, all those thousands of years ago.

There are still **Wolves** in North America, Siberia and parts of Europe.

The two most common types are the **Timber Wolf** and the **Arctic Wolf**.

Coyotes are found in the South-west of America.

In some areas Coyotes and domesticated dogs have bred giving a new breed, the **Coydog**.

Jackals still live in Asia, North America and Europe. Jackals have been known to attack men.

The **Asiatic Dhole** is a large, vicious dog with a red coat.

A Dhole will attack the large Asian Buffalo which is 10 times as big as itself!

The Dhole can be found all the way from Siberia to India.

The **Hyena** is still found in the Near East and in India.

The Hyena hunts alone, usually at night, and it feeds on any animal remains it can find.

The **Dingo** is the wild dog of Australia.

Dingos originally came from Asia, but were brought by the aborigines to Australia thousands of years ago.

Dingos are a great problem to the sheep farmers in Australia.

The dog was the first wild animal to be tamed by man, and he has been 'man's best friend' ever since.

BUT . . . like most 'best' friends they can be tiresome, annoying, irritating, time consuming, snappy, bouncy, jumpy, chewy, impatient, headstrong, bitey, smelly, muddy, over energetic and a bottomless food pit!

BUT . . . they can also be tender, loving, affectionate, sympathetic, cute, cuddly, tickley, licky, waggy, smiley, and when your dog puts his wet nose in your hand when you are least expecting it, you know that you have a friendship that will last a lifetime.